A Time When I So Loved Someone

A Time When I So Loved Someone

Poems of Lee Byung Ryul

Translated by Cho Young Shil

Homa & Sekey Books
Paramus, New Jersey

Library of Congress Cataloging-in-Publication Data
Names: Yi, Pyŏng-nyul, 1967- author. | Cho, Yŏng-sil, translator.
Title: A time when I so loved someone : poems of Lee Byung Ryul /
    translated by Cho Young Shil.
Other titles: Nugun'ga rŭl it'orok sarang han chŏk (Compilation).
English
Description: First edition. | Paramus, New Jersey : Homa & Sekey
Books, 2025.
Identifiers: LCCN 2025000796 | ISBN 9781622461264 (paperback)
Subjects: LCSH: Yi, Pyŏng-nyul, 1967---Translations into English. |
LCGFT: Poetry.
Classification: LCC PL992.9.P955 N8413 2025 | DDC
    895.71/4--dc23/eng/20250114
LC record available at https://lccn.loc.gov/2025000796

Published by Homa & Sekey Books
3rd Floor, North Tower
Mack-Cali Center III
140 E. Ridgewood Ave.
Paramus, NJ 07652

Tel: 201-261-8810, 800-870-HOMA
Fax: 201-261-8890
Email: info@homabooks.com
Website: www.homabooks.com

Printed in the USA
1 3 5 7 9 10 8 6 4 2

Author's Note

Upon receiving a poetry book publishing proposal, I
   took off to where it was snowing
Burrowed in the snow, I remained in the snow past
   the day scheduled to return
Then sprang to my mind the title for this poetry book
At the same time I drank in the scent of snow,
   woefully longing for the scent of snow

Such is poetry
Such is love

One who dances with a purpose to dance
and one who dances unwittingly;
all this malady of mine, if I should divulge, belongs in
   the latter

April 2024
Lee Byung Ryul

Contents

Part 1

A CERTAIN PAINTING

The two of the art gallery each
had a duty to guard this room and that, that room
   and this

Keeping people from touching the paintings
the distance between the two narrowed
Each of them fixated on the other
till they went on headlong to touch and caress

They both had their own space to tend
but they walked abreast over the whole space
never turning loose the clasp of their hands

A painting followed them around

Saying they will be inserted in it
the painting treaded on the heels of the two

CLOSING TIME AT THE PARK

These two only remained
and the rest scattered in every direction
Then the two take the same road

It would be fine should someone initiate the talk
but no one does and
no one deflects the road

These are the two that just got out of a meeting
Always the same members
and the leader picked daily seems to decide on the
    topic

In one meeting they washed hands clean and
    nibbled on bread

in another arranged lilies high and gazed up

in still another mixed, interposed the last and the
    first sentences of a book

and called by any name the shoots just sprung out,
    and so on

Are they musing on a situation where they oppose
    each other or mismatch
or the temperature there differs
therefore could not be wiped out or cut off
or blend despite much effort, I wonder

Two trees born apart drawing each other close

to build a wall, to let flow waters
and mutual inspirations interlocking
for no one to unravel;
I hear that is life in its entirety, nonetheless

dubious somebody could ever clarify the meaning,
dull night mingled with night
and unsteady footfall mingled with footfall,
we finally came to the front of the park   .

Lights at the park were going out one by one

DIRECTIVE

One hope for my future: let me get lost often

Being one who's never gotten lost
when I seem lost I just turn right around and find
   my way
or draw on the ground the return way
then easily get out of the deadlock
So please let me forever lose that bad habit

One hope for my future: to die often

Even if I die away each time faced with wreckage
   or disgrace
to fold me up and mend
let me not be born
Just this once then let me not cross with life ever
   again

Now one hope for my future:

to let whatever I put in a vessel leak again and again

to spill out what's on my mind each time I will put
   in something
to forget what time it is now
struck against a rock each time I fill up to the brim
Never to be shocked at the strangeness of life

LONG SINCE

In building a house he must have used wind only

The house a spider has built
between a tree and another
between a branch and another
between a void and another

I understand well enough but it's ever so far and
    tenuous and very long

Compared to the spider's boredom
the amount of his poison is perhaps not much of
    surprise

How is he doing
I remembered the spider transparent all the way
    through his inside
thanks to the light going through the body's front
    and back

So, apologetically and yet unapologetically, I
left myself hanging on the spiderweb solitary

I wonder if I am swinging
if I am drying fine

How will the world sustain itself without the
    spiderweb

Between a tree and another
between a building and another

between a void and another

the cobweb desperately holing on tight

EVERYONE'S AFFAIRS WE WILL LEARN SOMETIME

People are ready to misunderstand love
Ready, I say, to warp it bad or be jealous
I have begun to love Love
and am private

I am not always desirous of tasty food
For under the presumption of having insipid or
    unsavory food
fault with love will be born

Peanuts are what a stalk after flowering burrows
    underground and bears
Different views to take it as the stalk or the root
For all that, Love continues to be puzzled before me

Love may not turn up for our rendezvous
For I love Love
and Love reasonably misunderstands me
It's all very well just to count the soaring geese then
    come back

I do not so much like the summer season, rather
    dislike it
I do not so much like the magician job, rather dislike
    it
I've long since been rigidly convinced that my likes
    have codes
but not my dislikes

If we do not sense love
I am afraid we cannot crack this life's codes
so then how do we live like this

Is it that love is even in the rear end

THE BELL

In the cathedral rang out the bell

Hearing the bell, the neighboring village cathedral
  rang theirs
and kept time nearly as good to make harmony
Another village, on hearing it, chimes in
ringing their enormous bell, assisting the one in
  the neighboring village

As if nudged, the next village
and the neighboring one where the bell was heard
ring it in harmony though it was not the usual
  hour,
assisting in making music with bells
As people were steeped one by one in that tolling
one by one more people began to cry

Were this sound heard high in the sky
it would possibly be a great reason
to find out who you are and why you were born

No other way but this to tell you
that if you never listen in the sky
you shall go on living without ever knowing
the fact there is a music bound with thread

LINE

Seeing people in lines, I too joined
I didn't know where they were heading for and
   why, but that was alright

Seeing people going in flocks, I too joined
Didn't know their reason but just followed them

Often it was neither in front of a masterpiece
nor for a prearranged colossal plan, as they said;
they got in the line, cutting in if need be

One line gradually broke into a whole new line

Helpless, but I did not return
It became a line of no return once you were in
Eventually not one stayed but myself standing
   alone

DENSENESS

Light comes to shine in your eyes
Such is love

My own figure too has appeared
in the landscape reflected in your eyes
Such is love

World's many frames
spontaneously
have come to fall into place

When stars sway in the wind
I've come to believe your eyes just swayed

TRAIN TICKET

He that asked me out to dinner this evening
hands me a train ticket when we part

He says this morning he got a book from the bookcase
and found a train ticket he used long, long ago and kept

Says he wanted to give me something;
a train ticket with a date 6 years ago, the departure point
    and destination in a city of Germany, a far country

Von (Departure): Dresden
Nach (Destination): Leipzig

On my way out with the train ticket, determined to use
    it as a bookmark
wondering how the ticket might as well be used
standing long in front of the railroad's semaphore for
    no reason, looking for the delaying train
thinking of a few faces I need to love more

thinking the departure date on the ticket might be
    tomorrow, morning hour to boot,
 I drew near the street light, got it out to check

Uncertain whether I will have to whisper word
that I will vanish tomorrow not to return ever
I took out the train ticket, read in the street light

Von (Departure): Here
Nach (Destination): Eternity

13

GIDDY

I tell you snow melts to come to cherry flowers

I tell you cherry flowers melt to run in river water

I tell you river water freezes into snow

I tell you snow comes to cherry flowers to fly away
pitiful

I tell you wayward heart spills over

I tell you I want to be good to you

SNOWSTORM

They are crying, clinging to each other

Crying to no end in each other's arms

Not turning loose

Clinging to each other on their foot not to tumble
down

clinging to each other on the brink of tumbling
down together

Toe caps of the two are getting tear-sodden

Where the two stand in embrace

snow falls in heaps but away from them

as though touched by the heat and air

LIKEWISE

I meet a man
who says he's going to be a nobody

I ponder if he has ever weathered a storm

Being one akin to most people
who want to be nobodies

he does not bide his time
has no hint of smile
does not look forward to the next season

Yet it suffices
Thanks to the fact that they carry no weight,
the earth meanwhile will simply switch the place
   once

and likewise
no different from an ordinary daybreak
a tinge of love will break forth

Love will take a few steps on her own
each to be barely connected to each in solitude

PROBABILITY TODAY

It's unusual that I got water to dip myself in the
    morning
I watched the speed of a sliding soap
and the speed of its dropping to the floor

There are things opening and closing on their own
You see, a hanging bathroom tissue unrolls all on
    its own
or a rock at a standstill begins to roll

Solitude during the bath was brief
and I wrestled with the zipper on my jumper
neither going down nor going up all morning

There in front of the window kept open
is one last apple

In the backseat of the car I borrowed from a
    friend
is gift wrap of about 1 meter long rolled up

A voice said he waited long for today
I don't know if I misheard

How far have you come
It seems I'll be there a bit early

Part 2

A TIME WHEN I SO LOVED SOMEONE

A time when I so loved someone
A time when I senselessly grumbled for food in
    front of a plant withering to death
A time when I cried at the train station
A time when I didn't seem to care much
even if this feeling was an illness to be ridiculed for
A time when day by day there was little sunlight
    and I didn't have enough of you
A time when I wondered if I could go on liking
    and so thought up my qualifications
A time when I imitated one and ardently agreed
A time when I lost faith that baffled me from
    knowing what to do
and that I have it in me to change
A time when I seized eternity
that must have first reached where you and I
    finally left

TO YOUTH

And then I will get lost
Since there'll be nothing much in the bag
I will not use a thing like bag wheels
Only travelers won't know but the fact is
that in travel I will be a visitor

A few days' time zone with borders naturally
 crossed out
Depression swooping down on me at the speed
 of autumn leaves
Perhaps I am oblivious of the fact that I don't
 have to run
in a safety zone regardless of the concept of
 inadequate happiness

The better one maintains his temperature, the
 better off he can be
No one sees but for consideration of myself
it will be better that I dance my own dance

And then you'll arrive at a shop with nothing
 displayed,
lit up in the daytime, the door kept unlocked
The refrigerator still running, if you'd like a
 change of mood by opening its door wide, it'll
 work
You're entitled to a travel only after the day you
 try to step way behind
those who strive to come near something, and
 feet slipping, you're in calm air

20

If resolute for a traveler's life regardless, you
    should keep losing
It's okay to be sloppy once you are on the road
    again with nothing to win, no business to win

It'll be just me persisting in parentheses even
    when all's ended
and yet there'll be none other to fasten my heart
    to

Life will be intelligible if I do not return
after I get lost again
so I wouldn't feel too bad and
would spend an inconsistent life
Resolved that there will be no other road but this

PLEASE UNWIND THE CLOCK, AND SHAKE

If you shake the clock you won't see me
I will go on my way as I wish
and see the morning as I have never seen

Please shake the clock
even if you have to hang it on a bough
Then all living things will enter into the void
    between air and air, to a slow stoppage
Even thousands of downy hair will stop

All of it till now as we couldn't live without time,
I will reconcile myself that it never happened

If there remains strength in me I'll remove my
    necklace and wave
Watching blankly the weight of necklace, you will
    stiffen
and I will face you with the strength I had in my
    silence;
I will be kind and tender
the way one brushes off spiderweb with a long
    brush

Please shake the clock

When I fall into this sleep
dear you, please stay far away

I fall asleep but you from afar,

please collect the words you haven't uttered to me
and then get away from clouds

Now that I am awake to myself very slowly

I will get into sleep
to go ahead and commit the sins I dared not before

I will grind silence, float it away
and send my body alone,
my body in repose

so when I fall asleep, please tell me many a tale
Say that you will tell me all, nothing left

LOVE

Why do I not mind what someone says
but feel like death at what someone else says

Why should someone not touch me
but someone else may

Someone approaches me rough, giving me hard
    time
but someone else seems to hide self behind the
    rough

Why am I willing to be shot by someone's bullet
but want to dodge someone else'

Why does it seem alright if someone's teeth bite me
    to death
but unfair if someone else' chew me up to death

Will I jab you in the eye
Will you jab me in mine

I will entrust you with my portion of courage and
    sequence

LOVE

Even without a foot to step forward
or a hand to pull

Even without two feet
or two hands

Even if all are utterly gone, paralyzed

And even if you have no fervent desire
for you have nothing wherewith you will graft every
joint

HUMAN ORANGE

It's about a fist size
and in autumn hangs down for the mass

Less fragrant than peony, yet the richness
    unrivalled,
it ripens time and again, at last to bear bowels

Drawing in the rind, it fastens a nest
Simply bowing its head often
it has no intention to part from the outer world
and enjoys binding self to the branch

Maybe it just intends to leave an expression mutely
yet with a harvest of well over hundreds a year
no proper prop will hold up the house

Enjoying intertwining with each other
then dripping fruit sap, it sees fit to spread out
    somehow

Hoping for flowers in June when nothing happens
    to a lone body
and relishing hard frost on the lone body,
alone to bring all that into sheer gold

And so, that winter I became thousands of oranges

I WILL WATCH YOUR HOME

I will watch your home
A shabby home
A home with lots of plants
A home which does not stay occupied long

You see, I am considering living there

I will watch the future of your home
A home which may creak or hobble anyhow
An empty home a cat will guard
A home dust will silently alight on

A world shrieking and howling is coming

A home with no more moisture, its dryness even
    to tumble to nothing
I don't intend to pretend to watch your home
but to be a part of it

What do you think of me, who will beg my bread
by finding in the refrigerator foods past expiration
    date
The home in my arms, it will be warmed quickly
    by my body heat
One has to let something happen to the home

A home has to be understood by someone
Everyone thinks the same thing when entering
    one

Interviewing about the stuff at home, about being
   unable to find the existent stuff
will be my job to perform

Make a key for me
I will strive to maintain charm for a significant
   place
For what we need is light

THE SEA YOU WANTED

You are standing, looking on the crepuscular sea
I know you will not await stars in the dark
but focus on sides and angles that are slim

Looking on the flotsam and jetsam
speculating there are a great many deplorables
    inside you
you positioned the sea slightly upward

You've gone before to a river to scream every day
assuming a volcano is a volcano only when tearing
    the heart and shouting
Taken by a waterfowl, wings outspread as you
    looked up from the river, you followed
and learned the sea is not far away
Before that, I gather, you were standing in front of
    a pond

You let the sea come up with a supposition, If you
    were born again,
and at that hour you go to the sea to taste that
You go to the sea where things deserted today float
    right back
and think what you cannot cope with are deserted,
    nobody knowing,
and that is perhaps for the instinct not to leave
    fingerprints behind

MIDDAY MOON

It was the day I mischievously stole a persimmon
On the way back in an expressway bus
which stopped suddenly, with a bang,
the stolen persimmon rolled on

To some extent, because it was back seat
and there were many on board,
they were not likely to take heed of me
yet I could not help taking heed of them

An elderly man across from the vacant seat beside
    me,
probably noticing the persimmon which dropped
    to the floor when the suitcase tilted,
seemed to take heed all the more

The persimmon too is on a trip

So thinking, eyes closed, I dozed off
The bus felt nearing the destination, I was about to
    open my eyes,
the elderly man sitting on the third seat over
    reached out, dabbed me, pointed at something:

there at my feet was the persimmon
come back quietly to a halt and gazing up at me

ONE MONTH

You who clipped my fingernails just once left a few
    days later

and I didn't mind when I clipped them the next
    time

but then when I had to clip them yet again

questions came up: *Why do they grow back after you clip*
    them

It's fine that they grow, but why do I have to clip them off
    again

Suppose a thing did graze by me, then what was it,

is it that I still have residue since I alone have so
    much

As though announcing to me that one month has
    elapsed

the half-moon of fingernail rising up unstoppable

TAIL

The reason why a four-footed animal
has a tail is

to let him fold his four legs for a while
before a nice landscape
and look on, sitting on his tail as it happens

The reason why a four-footed animal
has a tail is

to let him wait for waiting
with his tail spread out, fancied to be wings,
when he is urgently waiting for something

to let him bear in mind his fate to sit on a
    thousand-*ri**
in a sunny place
and wait for ten thousand-*ri*

*1 *ri* equals 4 km.

WIND AND PAPER-BAG

The thing that favors a windy day most, a paper-bag

A paper-bag with nothing inside
blowing all it wants
nose-diving at will
bursting out laughing
plops and splashes, drowned in tears too

Banging into anything at random
collecting plumes, gathering seeds
and spilling them all along

Things that are nothings, I say, are truly impeccable

I KNOW

"I know you. Know who you are."

The person who wrote the words neatly and showed
        me
quickly crumpled the paper, put in his mouth, and
        chewed
as my eyes followed the sentence

The paper in his mouth
will be torn, ink smeared, making tooth marks

And somehow he swallowed the paper

Who am I as he knows
and that the fact is more or less definite
and the whole of it is digested in him like a pill

Instinctively I contemplated my being alive

What he says he knows is perhaps
me as he wants

But no need there, already I am no more

I believe surely there's something at the end of this
        world
so I want to act contrary, if ill-willed, to what he
        knows
Otherwise a small portion will be disclosed
and he may painstakingly venture to find more

I wished to conceal earlier
but I don't think I can hide any longer

"I know. Know that I don't know who I am."
I know I don't even have dexterity enough to put in
    my mouth the paper I wrote so, and chew it

At one end of a scale
I put Responsibility since I am responsible to find
    what's in the end of this world,
roped myself to the other end
and then waited till the rope broke
I had to wait to see if there's any more to break
    even if the rope eventually breaks

Actually, for a few days about that time
I contemplated my being in a world already dead

SHIP OF LOSS

People aboard the ship were silent
So was the person steering the ship,
their eyes didn't meet

It was not known where they were heading for
but the fact was that they all had lost their sweethearts

They are on the way to get a picture frame
There's nothing in the picture frame but a frame

A picture frame which freezes everything as it is,
when put into the frame

The ship sailing to load empty picture frames,
in which painful events, untouched, become pains,
sets sail in front of the canal once a day at noon

They are going to receive an empty picture frame
        each,
not knowing what to put in
and maybe good enough just to peer and watch
Some wish the ship would not return
and all this come to an end,
with an intent to keep all that hung in the picture
        frame for the time being

But those who went to receive the picture frame end
        up in shock
For there were empty picture frames piled high in a
        marsh

for they learn some came here to discard the picture
    frame
for they also learn they came to pick the picture
    frame someone had discarded

As a result every home
has a square mark where the picture frame was hung
    for long

THE FACT OF LONGTIME ACQUAINTACE WILL NOT KEEP A RELATIONSHIP

At first with malice I followed the friend
The spring in his steps alone
gave me enough kick out of stalking him

The friend walked into a house
A restaurant to be precise, and he locked the
    entrance from inside
Once inside, as he turned on all the interior lights
I held my breath, standing outside, the window
    between us
He walked into the inner part, started cooking

I didn't know what he was making, but he was
    intent
Time passed and I saw
Not even tasting the food he made
he discarded it into the trash can right away
That is, dumped it

The friend came out of the quarter
I began following him again
I don't know if my shadow outran him
He whirled round to a stop, to my surprise
From when did he sense he was being shadowed
A murderous fist swung toward me, anything but a
    longstanding friendship

As I resisted his fist, he motioned to say a word
   but hushed up

If three cannot love together
then at least two should be left alone to love,
but I am going like this

Your secret and my love are on extension
That's it

On the verge of saying *Isn't it lucky that I'm in a*
   mindset to resolve everything
and then *I don't seem to be able to drop out of all this*
   suddenly
like a snowstorm I gathered the friend in my arms

COMPLETE RECITAL

A little over three hours for reading in turn the
    poetry book *A TIME WHEN I SO LOVED
    SOMEONE*

We attend the late night post-event
We will briefly hold onto each other

Once, upon reading poems I wrote, I almost
    stopped writing poetry
With respect to the hope in me

Today over there also sits a man who likes to toast
I wished to push away the wine glass coming at full
    speed each time I raised it, but I speak with
    some hypocrisy
"I'd like to brush by everyone living on this earth. If
    possible."

Like tide I am buoyed up with intoxication
"Who will stave off hard times?"
The person in a corner, his face poetic, talking then
    nodding himself
Even though what most of us repeat, cold soju in
    front us,
is like questions hardly irreversible however much
    you roll up your sleeves

by turns we read a piece of poem each and
    completed the recital, even so,

each time it's for us to live on thus repressing
    yesterday's feelings

All are in a state of mind as though swimming the
    night
I guess I feel like racing in the wind alone
for I am rather inclined to liberate all of us thence

MARK

When the love is over
I am appalled that I was in love with a scumbag

That took place several times

To me becoming the worse scum
the more I love,
the fact that garbage piles up as garbage
even if snow streaks down in sheets
and stars in the night sky draw a veil over that place
was buried in oblivion terribly and simply

We live unaware that the needles we fit our lives in
    pile up rusted
Live unaware that the arrows we drew toward
    Beauty didn't hit the mark
and just lie there scattered

When the love is over
instead of being reticent
I go about mad, now a speaker of a foreign
    language

How many times did I stand back appalled at my
    love so insignificant

TO THE BODY

If I must walk an hour with eyes closed
as duty or punishment

then no occasion to walk backward

and if stalking someone, I am likely to lose him
and will never see one
who must walk with eyes closed like me

If I must keep standing as a tree
an hour a day like some absolute being

I will be scratched at once
by the light that shines deep into me standing so

and will encounter me one-legged
and break silence greeting myself for the first time

if I therefore could strip myself
just once a day
so in my whole body there'll be left no more words
    to utter

SCENT OF EARTH

A new grave has turned up
It came about one morning
People thought somebody must be buried in it

People in the neighborhood understood nobody
    owned the land,
but seeing the new grave
whispered there may be an owner now

Grass grew and time flew
There came a man that said nobody is buried in it
It was the very one who scooped up and carried
    earth to mound over the grave
He said there was one person he wished to shut in
    there

On hearing that, each recalled the one whom they
    wished to shut in

Soon they all sprang on and started digging up the
    grave
There came about a hollow

Someone asked if he might lie down to see how
    bad it is in there
It was a question unlikely to expect a reply
They took turns lying down in the hollow then
    coming out

Crawling out of the grave, someone murmured

that at the end of death even the electricity goes out
Someone else said that the body ought to be buried
    deep enough
so no more ghost should be left in the world

There'll be a day when the scent of earth will be
    longed for
Entering a room as much scooped out as life's
    volume
just once in life
one will actually lie down expecting an encounter
    with oneself

Shaking off earth, I too murmured

IN THE SHADOW OF A ROSE TREE

Suddenly a woman embraced a man
The man started sobbing
The woman thought to herself:

Something's happening to this man

Closer to her the man pressed
He then started sobbing
He quietly thought:

What has happened to me

TINGED LEAF

You must confess by the 32nd

Afterwards you may move to the next star

All the world's first loves, I tell you, cannot be
    fulfilled because of that person

Then, or later, do not reproach yourself

Part 3

THE SNOWS OF KILIMANJARO

Maybe seen in June 6 (Monday) 2009 news
I dated and wrote down that the icecap covering
  Kilimanjaro, Africa, would all but disappear in
  2015,
that it's melting 300 m3 per month

Again, on October 19, 2018
I jotted down the article stating that by 2024 the
  icecap on Kilimanjaro, Africa, would totally
  disappear

Why did I write these articles in two different
  notebooks

Was it in place of the sentence that should say
Where could I go

THOUGH THEY SAY EVERYONE GOES TO THE SEA

The instructor told me to see him in the studio
He said there's an attic above the studio
but it rang hollow

Through the window chinks at the place visited by
    someone lately
the previous person's scent was fading
Dyestuffs smelled as before

A thing like a person's trace
is to linger on through time
Even if it be fragments crumbling from intuitions

Maybe someone I may know paid a visit,
his scent afloat is now fading
I felt like crying but forbore with difficulty
for that person's scent and the instructor's was
    overlapping

Now to depart from the world the instructor
is going to call up one by one to share his paintings
I think the list includes someone I know
and some names he emulated but could not see in
    person

He who didn't carry with him lowly and ignoble
    excitement
but never once quashed his desires
was a man in need of storm

Also a man whose back was always sweaty wet for
much toil

As I expected he didn't show me the attic

Henceforth he will flow down into eclipse
When the time comes I too will
and leave a separate time behind

Diverse weeds grew together amid the grass in
courtyard
The snow unmelted on the distant mountain
reflected some light,
keeping the wide space in front of the studio

Being ignorant of how we were born and have
come thus far, how can we manage this thing
called parting
Though they say everyone flows down to the sea in
the end
perhaps the sea is not the end

NO WAY TO SHAKE AWAY, ALL IS IN BETWEEN

In combining water, element 1, and fire, element 2
there are things that are non-miscible
Just as the two will be separated only after something
    goes through

In Paris an ambulance is allowed to pass
only between lane 1 & lane 2
Those who use these lanes
should absolutely consider the fact that an ambulance
    may come;
they also think souls dash out in between

When falling off a precipice in each other's arms
we must see that we may end up between road 1 &
    road 2

When ordering a meal as well, we must accept the fact
that something between 1 & 2 is possible
Between 1 & 2, so to speak, runs sensation

Maybe life is to piece together sundries and press hard
yet surely death is an overnight affair,
now I grasp that if the former is 1, the latter may be 2

I suppose we will take care of our affairs in death too
For overcoming the chasm between 1 & 2
was a battle within the scope of life

Always patronizingly thrusting out 2 when asked for 1

Sternly proving the things
diminishing or leaking, for being alive

Who in the world severed 1 & 2, keeping suspended
apart

Supposing things of the world must be equal in the
night
so the drawer named A Day will close
one must consider taking off the cap in his brain
Taking off one's cap, then hanging it up,
I suppose that falls between 1 & 2

A BUNDLE OF SCRAP PAPER

Seeing a person dragging a sackful of scrap paper
a man feeling that person is dragging a casket
and another thinking that person is pulling love

and a man saying he'd like to follow the sack
and another not knowing that's a bundle of scrap
    paper, and so on

Seeing a man struggling to drag collected papers
you must not take him doing that
desirous of being carried on it
and sent somewhere

Please don't just discard, thinking you messed up
    your letter
There's one who collects all those to use for a
    mattress
It's quite terrible of him never to return them

If so, is that a mattress being dragged over there

Even if that looks like a mattress
the full inside stuff may be something else
which we cannot imagine
Who knows if that may be
what blotted out the full story or something

On the other side of the paper are
tracks of a biography, calm or passion or what not
wholly suffused

to remain intact all together

Therefore, please don't try to write anything
on the back of a person

BIRTH OF UMBRELLA

Would you please listen to my poem,
a poet takes hold of passers-by

The paper with a printed poem in his hand,
letters smeared here and there,
in the sun shielding his forehead with it

like a butterfly the poet perches on people's
    shoulders
or trips them up as if dancing

Clattering as when going over a speed bump on the
    road
those willingly held by the poet eager to read his
    poem to them

I wrote a poem like this
I'd like to give you this one, will you buy it?

Giving the poet a hug after hearing it through, a
    young man
opens his wallet as though reminded, gives money,
    then leaves;

just then it showers
An umbrella in one hand
walking with a piece of poem over head
perhaps apprehensive it may get wet, the young man

goes somewhere under his umbrella, yet another
over his head

LIFE HISTORY

I bone the fish, prop the bones against the edge of
    a hollow plate

The bones off the fish stand calmly, transformed
    into the word "poetry"

It's laudable of them not to have gone down my
    throat

not to drop while I transfer them to the plate

but to hold out that firm as poetry

So it is that one day I was bitten by something

That something was entirely poetry,

whose venomous tooth stuck in me

still not dropping out;

and so my life history is

that I had my hands deep in the river water

to catch something

TO A YOUNG POET

Let flow
this clearness
this valley

Diffuse
with this gravity
with this wholeness

Give life to
flower buds
fruits

Let everyone drink
winds
and seas

Then beings will put down wings,
will make fire, roast rocks;

be filled with language, give birth to language
Turn yourself toward the feet you hear calling out
and be a bow, not an arrow

TO YOU WHO INTEND TO LEARN KOREAN FROM AFAR

Intending to learn letters, you are beautiful
I can tell you intend to go somewhere

Learn the word "water" and the word "door"

Spare the word "next"
and use often the word "tomorrow"

I perceive language makes happiness concrete
On that strength, I think, you will meet people
and smile like one that has first learned to smile

Chances to meet shy and mild people
will come along the fishing line

Words that cannot be conveyed can be breathed out

Sleep or awake, learn by heart
the sentence "Keep from the rain, not from snow"
and the statement "What's a dream?"
Keep in mind that voicing "It's strange" is not
    necessarily
a bad thing to say
I say that's what you blurt out contrary to your
    thought

Just as you cautiously lift with a forklift and rescue
a cat in danger at a construction site

just as snowflakes falling, melting on a predawn sea
kindly learn Korean

WHEN I LIE DOWN DEAD

The music composed by whoever, I hear,
was known for hundreds of years as composed by
    someone else,
until discovered later whose work it was

And I hear a certain composer announced a piece
    composed by himself
as by somebody else, rationalizing
that he was afraid of public evaluation

A writer, it is told, got public attention
only after publishing a book under a pseudonym,
as the world didn't look to him

but what I did nonetheless: be there quietly
as though a hand passing, a wind passing, is all
    there is,
right there as it so happened

No name attached, that *is* eternity,
which indeed is solely proper, in place

Though I get to live the world twofold
I cannot possess the whole of the two,
even if I possessed both, at best it amounts to
    inheriting an underline indifferent or secret

Today, after the rain,
grass is slowly drying

From the first till now drying

and the tears I shed at birth
are still drying

A WING ON ONE SIDE, ANOTHER ON THE OPPOSITE

Flowers are in bloom
That year flowers bloomed all at once, out of
    sequence, as if for the last time
Profusion of flowers terrified me for the first time

(It was in China Visiting an apartment of an
    acquaintance, you couldn't get out as the
    complex was blocked It was locked from the
    outside of the central gateway What could you
    do More and more areas were being blocked
    rapidly as swelling water)

Even then the world continued for a while
It was a world daring to teach the difference
    between opening a window and closing it

(That night I dreamed of getting blocked not in
    China, but in Korea; heard in terror someone
    endlessly mounting then dismounting along a
    flight of stairs; what oppressed me all the more
    at the time was the supposition, What if my
    world is blocked)

Like love nears the end, lives with an excess of
    luster were nearing the end
Feelings for absolute necessities melted down
    desperately
It was an awfully hot summer, all of us were
    abysmally dispirited just for the heat

(It was when we went to a hamlet in Iceland that the
   contagious disease was just about to reach a
   pandemic level; when you came out of the
   swimming pool after swimming, it occurred that
   the pool was abruptly blocked for contamina-
   tion Physical education class for neighboring
   school children that used the swimming pool
   was cancelled, and the denizens began to
   whisper)

Your breathing on me gave me a disease
What was it, why you of all people

Not even knowing that, I ached, had a dry throat,
   one wing on one side and another on the
   opposite oddly struck together
People's footsteps up and down the stairs all the
   same
Doorbell ringing and stillness as nobody opened
   the door
The least murmuring, practicing the end
Stories going on the air disjointed,
   boxes disclaimed because of miscommunication
   and misplaced addresses were discontinued

(God told us to pour out all tears He bid us purge
   the words held back during this period, and past
   foul words You knew of course and did that It
   had nothing to do with God)

In the dead of night we heard sounds
Sirens mingled with rain sound, and the speech
   saying Could we now block
And then we felt an earthquake

Afterward, people caught a cold straight, not
   knowing how and why it happened so
Though very ill, one hardly came round to the
   early stage

Later on, this cold more painful than a contagious
   disease, tougher and more interminable,
people casually decided to name it Air Cure

ANGUISH OVER THE PART

The woman, who insists that I copied from her
    blog verbatim
and therewith published the poetry book
    SNOWMAN INN, calls me
again today and gets into a blatant brawl

(Her phone number as received changed almost
    everyday; from sometime ago she cursed and
    swore over the pay phone all day, so I dragged
    out the time and asked the police to go to the
    phone booth she was using A cop reported that
    it proved fruitless because he was on duty at
    another phone booth)

That's the way it goes, I do my work
I am not weak only when I work

"I suppose I'll have to stop seeing you now."
The woman whom I've never seen before
erases, writes invectives directed at me in SNS,
    suspending herself in the air and performing
    acrobatics

(Once she went from one motel to another
    damaging all property, frequently wrote down
    my contact info on the mirror, came to an event
    with an intent to kill me but was ordered to go
    home for the absence of a lethal weapon)

That's the way it goes, I am stabbed all over

All I have to do is turn to myself ruthlessly

(It was after I experienced being stalked that I
  came to deliberate whether it'll work if I lift me
  up when I wish to insult me, to kill me)

The stalker elaborates over the phone where she
  was, what she did there, what made her upset at
  me
If I don't answer the phone, she calls instead some
  places connected to me, throws a fit for the day,
  tells me she's going to throw cyanide

The stalker is frequently reported that she acts in a
  very uncommon way
and when asked by the police:
Who are you?
she gives my name in reply
What's your phone number? She gives mine
Hardly a surprise

I suppose it's not just me whom she disturbs
  insanely
but I'd like to ask her to live, taking all dull parts
  time and again

This being the case, my part
is a bird whose wings are glued together
A passenger ship that, its course cut off, won't give
  a storm signal

The part anguished anew over when it'll end
  should I keep the role disregarding perpetual
  coercion even in this way

A WHIE BEAR EMERGED

I don't think people know it

A high school male student verbally abusive, ill-
     tempered,
never minding the person seated in front
even though I am coughing and my back hair's
     blowing,
I don't think he knows I wanted to call him names

And the fact that I really wanted to say hello to
     someone after a few moments
And then the foul fact that when I plucked my
     courage to say hello
that person didn't reply

Such a time, a white bear is smiling yonder
When I cannot figure if it's because of me or who
     else
that I am at a loss, then a white bear is smiling

The abusive language "Screw you" on a danger sign
     warning cliff on a mountain path, or
when someone, who constantly talks about money
     and bonds,
looks down on me
seeming to say With superior purpose, that doesn't
     matter

And when I happen to hate someone for my own
     fault

a white bear is smiling
That alone is likely the best for me,
a white bear is smiling, standing in the distant white
    snow streaks

If you come across a white bear
please imagine that I am not far off

If someone oppresses you with difference in
    positions, its pressures,
an attack with honesty ending up shaking head,
or with absurd sufficiency,
please congratulate with a whisper your abraded
    knees

Even if you have nothing to offer the white bear
    close at hand
do not shun the fact that he may be an angel doll
    you take along, joints threaded

I can tell you things human are connected, but not
    to be unraveled
Do not try to unravel, please sit on the edge of a
    stairway and wait for the white bear

THE TRAIN DEPARTS FROM QINGDAO

Probably without tickets, the mother and son have
  only one seat
At one glance you can tell the good son is ill
His aged mother hands him thermos bottle, then a
  cookie,
and again a boiled egg, but the son acts like he
  doesn't want any
It appears that his upper body was badly struck by
  something massive
The train stops at a station,
the ticket holder comes to the seat that the mother
  took for herself
and now she has to stand

Long is the road home

The mother pours hot water into a cup of instant
  noodles, takes it to her son, and this time he eats
  all
He gives his seat to his mother who says it's ok for
  her to stand
The mother already ails for her son standing without
  a stay
As it dawned on her, she takes out medication,
  makes him take it
Their bundled comforter on the overhead
  compartment is in place
but she has to go on looking for an empty seat again

Long is the road home

The son who changed the place awhile seems to
disappear somewhere, then calls up his mother
Perhaps he told her many seats are available in the
    front compartment
or asked to come over anyway, the aged mother
    hurries over
The two will sit facing each other, or side by side
The bundle of comforter on the overhead
    compartment curls up, pushed forward inch by
    inch

It feels like the train has on board only the two
    who must be exhausted from hospitalization and
    nursing
Turning, turning along the curved railroad, the
    train is looking forward to the prospects of life

Terribly smooth road will be long, but it'll be fine
    turning, turning farther along

FRIEND

1
Two people are walking over the river

From a distance you cannot see their faces well

One bends to relieve himself
The other pauses and waits for him

Yes

The one lagging behind, going to bathroom, raises
    himself and makes his pace
The other who slowed down hurries a bit, probably
    to keep up

Yes

You'd better keep up if you can, even if you must
    link this and that

2
It was a season for those who finished picking
    mushroom to worry about how wax-eye warblers
    will winter

I walked in the desert

Someone was on the same path although I didn't
    know whence he came

Another spoke to me but I didn't comprehend

Deep night, it felt like someone else was touching
my face under a blanket, but it wasn't a human
hand but the wind

My feet sank deep, but the desert path was good to
walk on account of that

DESCENDING A MOUNTAIN

"Just finished studying."

Seeing that the bundle of bedding a young man
  brought into the train was oversized, the
  trainman stopped him

"I mean I just left a temple."

Then the trainman replied:

"Even so, you should send large bundles by post."

"I did, this is the remainder. They told me, No
  more, so I brought it with me here."

If the bedding is all that's left after sending other
  stuff, then, I wonder if they're kitchen utensils,
  cutting board, that he sent

The bedding not fitting into the overhead
  compartment, the young man sat down, hugging
  his bundle

What a great schooling for him to have not only
  bedding and furniture to take after all the
  schooling, but also a place to go tireless

But supposing he has no proper place to go, what a
  great schooling all the same

HUMANS PRACTICE

An old man is squatting in the middle of a street
Not many cars there, but the street was for cars in
    every respect;
a close inspection showed all five lanes on this
    street were for cars

Fixing my eyes on the old man's back from inside
    the car, held by sign, I
wondered if something was wrong with the man
and yet it was obvious that he's not just sitting in a
    state of inertia

The sign changing, I skirted by
honking out of fear that the old man may be in
    danger anyway;
he cried fiercely not to blare out

The reason he first squatted down
was because he was stroking a puppy fallen down

Was he the owner of the puppy that could no
    longer walk for the heat
Or was it a stray puppy hit by a car and breathing
    its last

The inability to move a lump of something
perhaps comes from one's own weight after all

but might I overlap on this one scene

a fact that a few days ago I was on the verge of
    tears
over a sheet of paper unmoving, unable to take my
    eyes off,

a fact that I was worn out, burying one person in
    paper,
in a sheet of white paper at that

THE FIRST DAY I REMOVED THE BOY LABEL IN THE WORLD

The day I did my first side job
it was raining

and the boy, who in the process of discarding
    shredded paper
tipped scraps of paper over the ground,
was scolded by the printing shop owner
for taking a long time to pick up wet piece by piece

Having some time left on the way back to work after
    lunch,
he dropped by a stationery for no reason, picked a
    pen,
wrote in the blank column of paper

"Today it rained much."

Not only on the day I first went to work but also
    afterwards
driving rain outside the window continued

Why did the boy have to climb the ladder one day,
did the ladder's wood decay in several days' rain,
he pitched down into a spot steeper than where he
    climbed
And got grilled by the owner again that he did what
    was not bid

Things you mess up, things falling down,
alike in that none can avoid, were occurring one after
    another

A LINK CUT SHORT

A girl sold knitting wool
It was at a Ukrainian marketplace, the weather
  abnormal with over 40 degrees Celsius
I didn't ask why she's selling wool on this
  sweltering hot day
I bought wool
Implausible, but I imagined it would be good if I
  could fly, wrapped in wool, and throw myself
  down, preferably not on the ground but into
  some human arms
The market was in the middle of removing all signs
  under the pretext of groundwork
The girl's wool, if sold in the fresh windward side,
  will sell at least a little

The girl's eldest brother sold woolen gloves in the
  neighboring Georgia Sold till the age with no
  woolen gloves came Days no longer cold, and
  no hands touching hot stuff directly, gloves
  piled up high in the house Apart from the
  expectation that an age in need of gloves
  because the world was being covered in snow
  for a prolonged time, a rainy season has set in
  You could buy, and also pick up an umbrella
  Much warm rain brought much debt The girl
  unknitted her brother's unsold gloves, began to
  slowly reel as though setting back fruit to the
  core stripped of meat

I did not ask the girl in writing if she ever learned
    about love
I got the wool out of backpack again, gnawed off a
    fathom of it
Then wound it about my wrist thrice, made a
    motion for her to tie it up
I had no idea if what the wool wound was I myself
    or a bone of a wish
Maybe my wish couldn't be a large bundle of yarn,
    the bundle of wool dropped to the ground and
    rolled
I mused I'd better drag the feet of a junior soldier
    shot last night, and bind together with mine
    swollen during travel

SOMEBODY ASKED ME IF HE COULD BUY ME A DRINK

Somebody in the next seat asked me
if he could buy me a drink

For a man, said to be from Northern Europe, to
    speak to a stranger
is as good as his best overflowing
He said he comes from Sweden
Every bit of a Northern European, shoving a
    drinking straw in courage

As he told me he's twenty one
I considered asking him if I could buy for him
    instead, but I accepted a drink
Hearing this was the first time for him to talk with
    an Asian
did I pay attention to my talking, I wonder

He said he drank from his childhood
Jokingly I said You must've had vodka; he said
    Yeah, I did
He added that his grandmother made vodka at
    home,
which probably tasted different than people knew

I don't know but I suppose it was different
I can't imagine your grandmother at all
and yet beyond the mountain she points to, a brook
    flowing in front of your house, the air in the
    glass jar with candies, smoked fish hanging in

82

the barn, an army of ants swarming around wild
berry syrup spilled, snow on the neck of a liquor
jar kept outdoors a few days;
I wonder if the house with a loft you climbed to
sleep was a cabin

You said you were going on a very long journey
I asked if I could buy you a drink this time
The beginning is great and you as such are greater

It's a wonder that strangers meet and share pile of
small, petty stories
It's a greater marvel that strangers make promises
shortly after meeting

"I'll go see your grandmother. You go on with your
journey."

Tomorrow an internal war may break out from the
border
but as I am a man of my word
and believe I should solemnly keep my promise
over the matter for the person on the other side
of the earth

I will go and hold her hand
so, world, please cease the war

THE HEART, A FLOWER CRAB

It never dawned on me that when I think I do so
    sideways
Nor the fact that my name has the word *flower*
I seem apt to cut and sever everything, but it's only
    when rumor goads me
I severed my claws after a single use, so they must
    be still stuck to the object
I tend to step aside not quite leftward, but rather the
    other way
As the case may be, up-down-left-right upturns and
    comingles
I've built many hideouts, I am ready to hide often
Retreat is frequently followed by failure
The main issue is that I foam at mouth often, and
    repeatedly
Until death, I am not only unaware of my walking
    sideways
but also know not why in the world I go about
    huffing and puffing, my twin hands hoisted high

TO A BOY

A child that came to bathe with his father
The father washing hair and rinsing out lather,
the son squeezing away shampoo onto the father's
   hair

Nearly done rinsing
then squeezing some more;
nearly done rinsing
then squeezing still some more

I suppose when the child was very young
his father once shaved his head clean for a full
   growth later
Must have washed the hair of his growing son a
   few times,
curious about under the nose like one who's
   waiting for something,
sneaked a look way down below his belly button

One holding back laughter, the other washing off,
buttocks of the two go on quivering
As if to make a screen between the two
the steam seems to make echoes shyly

They say the Ainu, a tribe in the northern sea,
decorates a boy by tying beads to his front hair,
holds a rite to cut the hair end
setting beads apart when he succeeds in his first
   hunting,

child,
now that you've learned the world's sore spot
how about cutting off a bit of your hair end
and then floating it down the bath water

Part 4

CLIFF ON THE SEASIDE

A rock stays afloat above the waves lapping a
    coastal cliff
The rock's surface is whitish with barnacles and
    such like, glued fast for survival
I try to hold it deep in my eyes
but it's hard, for it often floats like water
Gazing down at it, I was abruptly saddened

Why are you sad, you asked

Why aren't you sad, I asked

I was about to say how can I not be sad,
for the seaside flowed all the way down here ten
    thousand years ago
and this rock rolled over piecemeal from a tall
    mountain
a thousand years ago, submerging here,
but all I did was pick up a pebble and hand over
    to you

ISN'T THIS ALL TO UNTIE THE KNOT

In sight was a tent over the river where nobody lived
Implausible it was
For nobody up to now could do so over there

The interior of the tent might show through, but
    nothing happens
What's strange is that the one tree growing at the
    tent site is gone now

The emergence of the tent engendered in me a
    tendency to expand
and a will to shrivel
Even to doubt how a human being crossed over
    there
was just like having a cat in my mind

Three or four times I endeavored to build a stone
    bridge
but it often washed out

I almost told them to throw a rock to the waterside a
    couple of times at the sight of me

I was worried if they wanted to cross over here but
    couldn't
and what if there were nothing but cliffs and shades
    beyond
And waited just for the moment when the tent is lit
    up first time
When I came to believe it's about time they and I

get to learn our mutual situations
I was shocked at the fact that it was simply an empty
tent

It was a little later
that I heard a report of people who pitch a tent and
then just leave

Supposing life's share is not to cross over but to leave
behind
a mere resolution to cross over will be considered a
journey

I will be back
Will have to affirm my penchant, the longer put off
the more inclined toward the far side of that river

SWING

And yet I will go on
Along with the fact that for you this world consists
    only of
stories I want to hear, and stories I want to tell

Summer, the cicatrix on your bare wrist
was like a plant stem
You said you were opening a wine bottle
The iron cutting you, I guess, was just jealous of
    your world
and so, what was not severed off all
signifies that we should accept our own places

I don't think we can say this helplessness,
    irrepressible,
is nothing more than a farrago

I wonder if pursuing you may not be the answer

You may be left to yourself
To clarify questions about yesterday's world,
    impure habits gnawing off that world,
 and why flowers are ever so red

So I will go on
And tell you I will sustain a world turned barely
    comely on meeting you
and if not today, it will likely crumble away

It may be that I wish to have you discover
my one-sidedness desperately licking this persistence

BROW MARK ON A STOREFRONT WINDOW

A brow mark on a storefront window

It was on its outer side
To peer at whom?
The brow pressing unawares while trying to say
    something?

The mark which couldn't find a way into the inner
    world
remains plain after a good while, never wiped out

When streets darken faint light streams from within
each time making the brow mark clearer

It isn't that the brow has the window mark
but that the window has the brow mark

and the mark, if allowed,
will likely remain till the window gets blasted to
    pieces

You never know if inside the brow mark
might be whirling
the whole of the soul muttering something to self

A very deep hour, the brow mark repeatedly
    surfacing
as bright car-lights pass by every now and then

onto that brow I overlapped mine
I didn't want anyone to detect
my absolute conviction that I could see well
    something inside
precisely by bringing the brows together

BRIEFLY, THE STORY OF A CURTAIN

Not a single one at first
but now so many slipping out of their clothes and
    then into laundered ones,
hence a story that they prepared a curtain
A story of a self-service laundromat

Whether in a hurry for something
whether that is a single thing to wear
CCTV often featured plainly
them taking out, then wearing just-dried clothes
so, the laundromat owner, considering to fix a
    mirror,
prepared a curtain along with a mirror,

a story that the story sounded like one supporting
    human substructure

Not because I recalled a newspaper article
about a man who got in an empty full-size washer
then caught sleeping all curled up

or because I remembered the warmth lingering long
    at my fingertip,
when I went to do my laundry, picked up one side
    of another's
which was left in the washer

yet talk about the world having a mind
to shield with a curtain, to reflect with a mirror;

a story that I wished to be the outer side of the
    curtain
to sway a few months or so

VENTILATION

1

The one I suddenly recalled when water got into
   my watch
because I didn't take it off when bathing

The one I recalled again
when the glass of the clock hanging on the floored
   room fogged up
because I didn't shut the door when bathing

So I kept looking out
Looked on and on even while working
Till the sun setting brings on darkness
my heart opens and shuts, then stoops, fearful of
   its fading away,
I must be suffering some sort of pleasure

After shaking my head over and over
I began to gather up keys
I tried to fit them one after another
into every chink of your world

2

Is it because I had this thought
When I returned home, the door I left locked is
   brazenly open
and the garbage can, someone entered the house
   and took it
The garbage can, taken by the one that burst in
   the house

without a search warrant, without assent

Not the odor
nor the loneliness
just the garbage can

What did I discard, I brood
but cannot remember what

neither can I chase my monologue
as I don't talk of myself at the house I alone live in

What did I put in the garbage can put aside, I
    wonder
Did that person kick me out even in this manner
Was the home invader personally in the right

POST OFFICE IN AUTUMN

Through the post office door, kept open, sweeps in
    a wind

Each time a wind sweeps in
a number ticket pops out, caught by the sensor of
    the waiting number machine

Each time a number ticket, pushed on, drops out
    like an autumn leaf
the waiting number above the postal clerk in duty
    switches
with a ding-dong
and the clerk rises to his feet with a Welcome!

Nobody comes to the post office in autumn

HOUSE-MOVING DAY

Have you ever changed your residence
Ever done
house-hunting by yourself
and the duty of moving by yourself

I tell you, there's no halfway feeling then
Only a definite emotion

What a grueling thing that is
To decide against what to lean a wobbly dining
     table up,
where to stack for now boxes of books whose
     bottoms slip off

This really is such a narrow square room
yet on the first evening and night it's not narrow at
     all

so happy and sad,
so all the more saddened

Having unloaded the furniture somehow
taking a walk around the village
I run across the lit business signs of a beauty shop,
     a noodle store
Just as such an array
you might have a plan to settle in sowing seeds by
     the window,
and a dampening uneasy feeling that life won't be
     good for you

yet an anticipation of a river not too far away
and a supposition that any boat could be launched
    on that river

even so, if you move your residence
and that, if you move and have to do everything by
    yourself
you shall know how I am living in exile
how useless trying to be holy
trying to cross out the previous residence

GIVES A NIGHT'S LODGING; PARTING IS EXTRA

There was nobody in the bus bound for the public square. So it was like sailing into a city. The person I was to meet, the owner of the home I was scheduled to stay at, was known to be blind. I was told he'd be standing with a stick in front of a statue in the square. It seemed he was to meet with the world by offering a couch in his house*. Which stood on the hill stretched along from the square.

During the three days of my stay there, his one impressive question among others was, "What kind of season is it in Korea now?" It smacked of a great anticipation, but I replied that it's just the same. When I said only flowers in bloom there are different, his ears cocked. He raised one hand over the Braille computer monitor. I wiped every inch of it with a wet tissue while he kept away his eyes.

There was a turtle sleeping under the sofa I slept in. He told me he and the turtle have lived together quite a while, and it crawled out when I opened the refrigerator door. It was unlikely that it wanted something to eat, but more likely cold air. When I opened a window, it, ordinarily munching a carrot, a lettuce, and suchlike, took the trouble to turn to crawl under the couch; I don't know whether in response to noises from outside or to light.

My three days' stay at that home as arranged came to an end. He insisted doggedly to see me off to the public square. Tap-tapping of the cane, rattle-rattling of the suitcase dragging filled the narrow downhill. I said You may get back now, and he said To come out to the square and sit every day is my goal. Goal.

What I could do for this friend is to let him stay a few days in my couch. Of course I have to buy a couch since I don't have one. I said Let's meet again in Korea, and added, "I make books and keep a plant store." Cocking his ears, momentarily he exuded an air of hope. "If I can only follow you right now, I could write in my chronicle that this is my very first travel..." He, who says he has never set a destination since he was born, waved long. Well, nothing to step on, he lifted his hand as high as he could. The motion delicately rippled out through his body. For the first time I thought he may not be blind.

*A concept known among travelers all over the globe as "Couch Surfing", it denotes a culture that gives the traveler a lodging on the couch in the home-owner's living room. It is contingent to mutual exchange of space if desired, with no charge, albeit between strangers.

I LIKE PIECES

I like fighting
but have no idea how well I can fight for I never
fought

I like writing poems
but have no idea how much for I am ever subject to it

I wanted to say
that the things I've liked alone from afar are virtually
palpable

I like to be moved by music
For it a day may be ruined, or I may be soothed
so I keep it on to no end

I told you
to engage in the task of making salt,
to produce salt enough to shake down
between creases of clothes, between folds of flesh,
not enough for food though

that such is the way for our bodies not to go below
zero degrees
that the fact you've come a long way and the
calculation you've a long way to go
is therefore a momentous accretion

I like railroads
for they stretch far toward truth
I like snakes

solely for wishing for an encounter

Liking what I like
liking the fact that seeds join to settle where they like

just as one red lump there is
which you look on slowly, gaze long,
bravely turn into a rose and bloom

just as a clear breath
drawn in for a long time grows into a dance
and one large apple I ate fully
in one day turns me an apple exactly alike

if I walk all day, holding the one I like
I gain the place I want to live, under a tree over the
    hill

Ah, I like to call myself
for I have no idea yet if that is possible at all
and how to call and then answer

WHAT I WANT

I was a substitute for one person
Seeing me, people took for him
I too pretended I was he
For I didn't hate it

What I could relish was a privilege, and myself

Have you ever been to a portrait gallery known to
     pick a backdrop for you
I was elated that I might live a different life simply
     with the backdrop

I liked to be asked questions
Just the fun to give relevant answers whose validity
     was dubious,
a luxurious feeling as on a business trip in new suits
     to an unknown country

I embarked on a ship
calculating I don't have to return

Whenever I thought it's alright to be me, or him
I, who hold the key I think could overturn life
     profile,
naturally assure myself to be him just once more

Maybe I became beautiful, too
Supposing the dignity of his beauty was what
     people wanted to pursue

I am laying my hands on an unexpected sense of
    being so well treated as to make me feel sorry

I stayed put and focused on simplicity, but even he
    was simple and so too, even he lost grit, hence
    this was a substitution I took on myself
Until when could I
keep this privilege and ecstasy in my skin

THE HEART LOATHING TO SEE

Two of us went to a Chinese restaurant, and no seat
    available, we were led to a room
Outside the window I could see trains coming and
    going

Sitting at the round table, looking at the inner table
    not to be spun,
I thought we two are alike
in that we look not in the least alike

Spinning in one direction the centerpiece
with a tea kettle on
I fancied the emotions laid on top of it would pick
    up speed

I think I too will take the train and return now
In between things static and things turning
were wedged fast something akin to time unmoving

Do you turn the spinning table like a wheel of
    fortune
By now the question would be whether it'll turn
but we two, having ordered nothing else but a pasta
    dish each,
do not see why we should keep turning the table

By eluding, I shall remain one with nothing to gain

I may have visited you in order to go farther away
but I must take a train

Something like the final will to gain that far place
   even if late

Everybody wants the last train
For that is the last darkness

I must take the last train
Otherwise I shall be left behind,
and the mind wondering what is the use being left
   crudely, densely

EXCLUSION

To go to Norway I bought a travel guidebook
I took my seat in the plane slated to take off, turned
    to the beginning of a book
and the plane was not considering a takeoff

They broadcast information with their apologies a
    few times
then suddenly served a meal
It was slated to take off at 12:am
but it was now 3:30 am
Stranded on the earth, in the plane at that, I was
    served much wine

After all the plane did not take off
All the passengers recovered their packages, had to
    move to a hotel
Again they notified in advance of midnight
    departure,
stated that close to boarding time each will be
    contacted in his room

Be it a secret room or a special guest room, there I
confined myself and did my best to wait for twenty
    hours

but an odd premonition struck me that I might be
    the only one that got no message in time
so I called the airline staff
He said: The plane is already moving along the
    airway

110

Do I have to stay in this room again
Is that on the bad side

The unused plane ticket was to be reimbursed
and it was a good thing I didn't have to spend my
    saved travel expenses,
nonetheless I was left behind
It occurred between 12:am and 0:00 am

AT THE AIRPORT

I saw those who take pictures
of the one walking farther away in parting
The two, as though they would do the best to each
    other,
pose far enough, phone in hands,
that's what they are doing in their sadness

For now it'll be inconvenient, still no other way but
    to split

After I reckoned there is a species that mutually take
    pictures when splitting
I was back at the airport once more

From the two bodies in parting, hugging tight then
    releasing
I heard a tree-branch splitting with a crack
It just so happened that the one pleadingly crying
    out
How in the world could you talk about leaving far away
    hugged the other
and a noise louder than a tree splitting open rang
    out through the airport

The two, startled at the noise even after taking their
    hands off each other,
just kept standing, unable to lower their two arms

There is a species which in parting lets out, with an
    air of finality, a noise of a tree being uprooted

Commentary

A Time When I Loved, a Time to Love

Lee Kwang-Ho
(Literary Critic)

To declare "There was a time when..." is similar to saying that there was a precedent of such a time. Time leaves no marks, and the clue to prove the existence of that time is material marks, rather than the heart. A lot of accounts of love attempt to show "then (there) was a love". How, then, can one testify to the heart's affair in those days? In order to complete the lament for the time of love, one has to presuppose the existence of that time. If the question is the evidence to prove that such a love did exist, the ontology of love after the loss stands on a certain token. By the token the absence of love is now made the time remaining. But can the material marks prove in itself the time of love? The material power proving that time has to rely on verbal power. Without language showing marks and remnant time, things themselves do not speak by themselves. Writing poetry is a work to restore the sensation of things, to read time and represent. As though recalling the subtle sensation touching love in that time is the way to attest to the existence of love in the past.

> A time when I so loved someone
> A time when I indecently grumbled for food in
>   front of a plant withering to death
> A time when I cried at the train station

A time when I didn't seem to care much
even if this feeling was an illness to be ridiculed for
A time when day after day sunlight was little and I
    didn't have enough of you
A time when I wondered if I could go on liking
    and so weighed my qualifications
A time when I imitated one and ardently agreed
A time when I lost faith that baffled me from
    knowing what to do
and that I have it in me to change
A time when I seized eternity
that must have first reached where you and I
    finally left
"A Time When I So Loved Someone"

In this poem appears "a time when I…" frequently.
What is curious above all is that the enumerated
phrases are not followed by a predicate. Here, "a time",
an incomplete noun, denotes a period when a certain
action occurred or a situation developed. In this poem
is only an enumeration of those "times" and not even
one sentence ends in complete form. A time when I
loved as goes in the poem does not reach a time when
I loved in record. Of course we can conjecture a
possible omission of "there was" prior to "a time
when"; and can also say it is a question of poetic
implication and rhythm. The omitted predicate,
however, unfolds a more subtle dimension than that.
"Someone" leaves room to take these "times" as "no
times". This can be termed poetic "latency" instead of
poetic license. Latency, to wit, is not a level of choice
between what have been materialized, but a situation
prior to the materialization, a circumstance uncertain
what is to emerge and transpire.

114

The omission of a predicate can bring about poetic efficacy in two contexts. First and foremost, it works to remind the reader of the sensation of that time without saying "there was a time when...". To put it in a radical way, when the contents of "a time when I ..." are elaborate and exquisite we come to think such an expression is a language solely for the one who had perceptive feelings, even though he writes, "no time when I ...". For example, since the expressions like "a time when I indecently grumbled for food in front of a plant withering to death," and "a time when day by day there was little sunlight and I didn't have enough of you" already testify to the existence of those times; hence these powerful images are presently conveyed even with a predicate "there was no time when...". Another context relates to the latency surrounding time in poetic language.

The omission of the predicate does not limit the "time when I..." simply to some time "in the past". Here, "a time when I..." is not limited to a literal past time; it is rather a name of the time now undisclosed but latent. Which is a "latent time" as a poetic moment. The time with no predicate signifies not the reality of merely a past experience, but is a sensation of a non-existent and yet latent time. Being able to verbalize this latent time, and provoking thoughts of a being's sensation in the frame of time means poetry writing. This poetic "time image" thus fires both sensation and memory, initiating another latent time. The final line subtly implies the contents of that "latent time."

A time when I seized eternity

that must have first reached where you and I
finally left

"Where you and I finally left" belongs to past tense, which cannot be completed because we have no way to know if they did reach "there". "That must have first reached" is associated with present perfect, or with present perfect progress, but the suppositional nuance in "must have" is not clear whether it is also a completed matter. "A time when I seized eternity" is close to the past, but hard to conclude so without a predicate. This sentence indicates an indefinite time between uncompleted past and present perfect progress. Is the remark "a time when I seized" viable when it's unclear if "eternity" first reached there indeed? If this sentence is about the eternity which "first reached" the ambiguity of tense may not have occurred. But the ambiguity in "must have first reached" throws open this poem's latent time into another dimension. In other words, "a time when I seized eternity" is not a past reality but a time "potential" yet uncertain. It will be difficult to conclude that "a time when I seized eternity" in an account of love is a past reality. Supposing eternity signifies a state continuing to no end into timelessness, transcending time, how can the statement "in the past I've seized eternity" stand? Poetry writing does not end in disclosing the logical absurdity, but goes further to invent a certain unknown time between "a time when I…" and "eternity." The omitted predicate and the open tense in this poem do not allow the love affair to simply remain a past reality. The love affair has no definite tense; it is an affair of "a past to come" and "a long-ago future."

Even without a foot to step forward
or without a hand to pull

Even without two feet
or without two hands

Even if all are utterly gone, paralyzed

And even if you have no fervent desire
for you have nothing whereby you will graft every
    joint
"Love"

The omission of the predicate creates a delicate
rhythm in this poem as well. Surprisingly devoid of a
sentential subject, the subject of the act and affairs are
also left open. What's reiterated in this poem is the
expression, "even without..." or "even if you have
no....". With a negative conjunction included in the
subordinative clause that goes "you have no...", one is
apt to guess that these sentences will probably be
followed by "there is..." or "... is possible". But
there's no way of knowing what can be "without...".
We might presume it is perhaps "love" for this poem's
title is that. The reality of love, however, is an
ambiguous concept, therefore "love" can be a thing
"made to be without...", rather than a possibility
"without...". What if the cause of the nonexistence of
"a foot to step forward" and "a hand to pull" and "two
feet" and "two hands", "all utterly gone, paralyzed",
and even of "fervent desire" is love? Wouldn't it be
natural to think that "love" is not something possible
"without...", but an event that "takes away..."?
Between the love as the cause of depletion and the love

still existing, between the paralysis as well as loss and yet "what is now" lies the latency of the thing called love.

> The two of the art gallery each
> had a duty to guard this room and that, that room
> and this
>
> Keeping people from touching the paintings
> the distance between the two narrowed
> Each of them fixated on the other
> till they went on headlong to touch and caress
>
> They both had their own space to tend
> but they walked abreast over the whole space
> never turning loose the clasp of their hands
>
> A painting followed them around
>
> Treaded on the heels of the two
> saying they will be inserted in it
> "A Certain Painting"

A certain love affair may be recorded this way. Stated in the third person past tense, this love account appears clear. But it is not easy for this account to be regarded as an actual past. An account of the two, who guarded the gallery's rooms in the care of each person, came to love and "walked abreast along the whole space", will be a viable one. However, the sentence that goes "a painting followed them around" gives this account of love a leap into another level. The translation of a love affair into an imaginative dimension establishes a realm inexplicable by the rhetoric called metaphor. The space where love happens in this poem is an art gallery. While a gallery is anonymous and accessible, open to the public, it is also a place of sharing private sensitivity in the context that they encounter paintings with the artists' distilled aesthetic senses. And a gallery requires not a forced adjustment to the rhythm and time on the screen as does a movie theater; an unknown encounter is within reach in that one has to find a viewing rhythm autonomously. If love is born therein, that space will transform time itself. If love is born between the two who each kept a different space in the art gallery, that space already enters into a different time. In regards to the exceptional time, this poem states "a painting followed the two". The time they reached in the different context is the time of love imaginative and latent. The starting point of this poem may not be "the two" but perhaps "a certain painting". We can assume that the desire of the painting to have the two "be inserted in it" has been fulfilled, and out of that painting flowed this imaginative love affair. Consequently, how can this love affair be shut up in the flat time "past"?

> Are they musing on a situation where they oppose
>   each other or mismatch
> or the temperature there differs
> therefore could not be wiped out or cut off
> or blend despite much effort, I wonder
>
> Two trees born apart drawing each other close
> to build a wall, to let flow waters
> and mutual inspirations interlocking
> for no one to unravel;

I hear that is life in its entirety nonetheless

dubious somebody could ever clarify the meaning,
dull night mingled with night,
unsteady footfall mingled with footfall,
we finally came to the front of the park

Lights at the park were going out one by one
From "Closing Time at the Park"

The incident in this poem proceeding in present or present perfect tense is relatively simple. Here are "the two that just got out of the meeting". "These two only remained / and the rest scattered in every direction" and then "the two take the same road". Neither of them says anything or "deflects the road". The love affair in this poem has not yet begun. Only, they are keeping walking the same road. The narrator in the poem 'relays' in a kindly tone the time of their walking together. Now the tale goes on and the narrator does not fully know the interior of the two, or the conclusion of this course. There is untold latency between "a situation where they could not blend despite much effort" and "mutual inspirations interlocking" in human world. That has not been decided to these two yet; only "dull night mingled with night" and "footfall mingled with footfall" then "we at last came to the front of the park". One can imagine, even after reading through this this poem, the time when the two reached the front of the park and thereafter. The time when "lights at the park going out one by one" is a very late time when the park should be closed, and the two will probably not be able to get inside the park. Time between persons as "dubious somebody could ever clarify the meaning" still remains unknown. Whereabouts is this poem's moment? The durational adverb "finally" denotes a completion of a situation, simultaneously announcing time has entered into another realm. Hence, finally, the "closing time at the park" is not simply a shut time but an 'initial stage' which leads us to imagine the unfolding of the unknown.

When the love is over
instead of being reticent
I go about mad, now a foreign language speaker

How many times did I stand back appalled at my
   love so
insignificant
From "Mark"

A time when I loved might be a story about that time. For example, there is a time "when the love is over / I am appalled that I was in love with a scumbag" or belatedly realize "me becoming the worse scum / the more I love". In this case the love affair can be remembered in perfect past tense. But the time of love as in "when the love is over" "I go about mad, now a speaker of a foreign language" is not completed. A love affair is one that changes the language and the way of existence by any means, and one that recurs. Being "appalled" then is not for just once but recurring 'a number of times'. Even severe regrets and aversion paradoxically show the love existed so, and recurs so. In that mishaps recur, the narrative of love is not to be completed easily.

If we do not sense love

I am afraid we cannot crack this life's codes
so then how do we live like this
Is it that love is even in the rear end
From "Everyone's Affairs We Will Learn
    Sometime"

There is no way to resolve misunderstandings and mishaps touching love. "People are ready to misunderstand love" and "love continues to be puzzled before me" and "love may not turn up for our rendezvous". "May not…" can be the most honest of rules of love. The number of love-related probability exists only as a negative one, which goes "may not be…". "My likes have codes / but not my dislikes" has a context that a reasonable basis for "my likes" cannot be stipulated. What's left is a sensation of love, which is the only key to crack "life's cords", and yet the question "how do we live like this" trails on. The last question, "is it that love is even in the rear end" inherently laments this fundamental mishap, but what matters will be the imagination about "the rear" induced by that persistent question. That one is in the love's "rear", not in the "front", is also a matter of one's mental vision and time. To turn the question of such a strange love's abode into something creative, it ultimately has to draw near to the realm of 'language / poetry writing'.

I wonder if pursuing you may not be the answer

You may be left to yourself
To clarify questions about yesterday's world,
    impure habits gnawing off that world,
and why flowers are ever so red

So I will go on
And tell you I will sustain a world turned barely
    comely on meeting you
and if not today, it will likely crumble away

It may be that I wish to have you discover
my one-sidedness desperately licking this
    persistence
From "Swing"

Opening the sentence with "I don't know if" is a
cordial dialogue style, meaning 'may do...' or 'may
be...'. It is articulated in a diffident tone, shy and short
of conviction. This tone makes engaging rhythm; the
poem's title being the "Swing", the rhythm may echo
the 'pendulum motion' of a swing. The "swing" may
also be a third person pronoun. And the speaker in his
diffident tone declares "if pursuing you may not be the
answer" and "so I will go on". If this poem's title is a
"swing" in pendulum movement, the act of "going on"
does not suit. Because a swing's pendulum movement
is a back-and-forth motion powered by a fixed axle.
Sentences which run "pursuing you" isn't the answer,
hence "you may be left to yourself" and therefore "I
will go on" point only to the endless attempts in the
dimension of back-and-forth motion. Because
pendulum motion, even though it cannot actually go,
is a continued attempt to 'go', only just to return. That
is a motion telling "I will sustain a world turned barely
comely on meeting you" and "if not today, that
sustaining will likely crumble away"; a motion desiring
"to have you discover / my one-sidedness desperately
licking this persistence". And a motion to have you

discover the declaration "I will go on", and the anxiety and misgivings that "if not today, I will likely crumble away".

Why are you sad, you asked

Why aren't you sad, I asked

I was about to say how can I not be sad,
for the seaside flowed all the way down here ten
     thousand years ago
and this rock rolled over piecemeal from a tall
     mountain
a thousand years ago, submerging here,
but all I did was pick up a pebble and hand over to
     you
From "Cliff on the Seaside"

The reason for his eruption of sadness near a cliff on the seaside was because he sensed the operation of remote time of "ten thousand years ago" and "a thousand years ago". To imagine what time immemorial has accomplished is to realize the 'swiftness' of one life. Contemplating 'swiftness' is dual, on the one hand reminding us of this life's fleeting nature, and on the other hand of this moment's compelling beauty. But the narrator does not elaborate to "you" the minutiae of his sadness. What he does instead is double-folded in context. A performance or ceremony of sorts in picking up "a pebble and hand over to you". This act is significant and dramatic. And then there's the poetic language with the narrator's hidden meaning coming to the surface. These two things were elected in place of 'telling you', both of them part and parcel of poetic expression. "Pick a pebble and hand it over" instead of giving the reasons directly, so to speak, can be called a poetic act.

> Now one hope for my future:
> to let whatever I put in a vessel leak again and
>   again
>
> to spill out what's on my mind each time I will put
>   in something
> to forget what time it is now
> struck against a rock each time I fill up to the brim
> Never to be shocked at the strangeness of life
> From "Directive"

This poem is titled "Directive", but in the text it is presented as "one hope", a shade humbler expression. The narrator's hopes are to "get lost often" and "die often", and to "let whatever I put in a vessel leak again and again". The attitude commonly manifested by these hopes, as it were, can be regarded as the rejection of accomplishment and maintenance of aims. When "whatever I put in a vessel leak again and again" is a hope, life goes to extinction and oblivion each moment instead of being accumulated. Because I "forget what time it is now" as coordinates in time, there's no need to "be shocked at the strangeness of life". To slightly rephrase it, such an attitude toward life is also an attitude toward poetry.

And so it is that one day I was bitten by something

That something was entirely poetry,

whose venomous teeth stuck in me

still not dropping out;

hence my life history is

that I had my hands deep in the river water

to catch something
From "Life History"

The world of Lee Byung Ryul delves into the time of love still in "the rear end", and into the inner personality with the moment-by-moment journeys etched therein. The time when love moved in this poem overlaps with the time poetry's venom bit him, and with the time of his becoming a poet. "The bones off the fish, transformed into the word poetry." "Bones" are also the medium for his poetry to stand fast. "Poetry whose venomous teeth stuck in me". Were poetry the "poisonous teeth", then what's "my life history" inescapable of it? "That I had my hands deep in the river water / to catch something" is not a very helpful means. Putting one's hands deep in running water to catch something hardly visible is a means with not that high a success rate. This act, neither efficient nor functional, is similar to "whatever I put in a vessel leak again and again" in the poem above. A time for the elusive and the leaking is the time of poetry / poet's "life history". Dipping one's hand in the river water to catch the elusive, and wishing not to hold anything is a poetic attitude tantamount to 'standing fast' toward essentially the unknown.

Suddenly a woman embraced a man
The man started sobbing
The woman thought to herself:

Something's happening to this man

Closer to her the man pressed
He then started sobbing
He quietly thought:

What has happened to me
"In the Shadow of a Rose Tree"

A scene like this can be a symbol of a love affair. Something, a tactile event, happened between two people. Suffice it to say that it's a sort of 'affectation', it is an event shaking the sensibility and skin and body. The problem is that something happened but you don't know what. Your skin quivers, your body sobs, yet you don't know the origin for yourself. That the incident of the trembling body remains unknown suggests the fact that the moment is 'latent'.

That is a 'feasible' scene, but there is no knowledge where it began and when it will recur. The subject of love thus abandons confident subjectivity itself, and throws himself into the other's world. Love will be "in the shadow of a rose tree" sobbing, unaware what has happened to her. Supposing the time when I loved is not an actual past but some latent time of love, a moment you do not know what just transpired is the moment 'when you will be in love', an event to come about. In that case I would think an actual time does not come first, but 'a burgeoning' love brings forth an unknown time.

There is a world of words hesitant, ambiguous, and stammering because the body senses a love affair has happened but cannot figure out its details. So, too, a world of words slackening for the inability to "crack life's codes". That slackness in words, however, can excel rather quick words in finding the rhythm of love possibly in the "rear end" of life. In her commentary of *Radiant* (Moonji Publishing Co., 2010), the poet Heo Soo Kyung writes: And this is Lee Byung Ryul. With his world so opaque, he is one poet who has experienced countless moments of slackness in his words. There is no way to disagree with her depiction, but I append one small thing: And this is Lee Byung Ryul. The very moment when he is slack in his words is the time when his heart's rhythm starts.

About the Author

Lee Byung Ryul, the poet, was born in Jecheon, North Chungcheong Province, and graduated from the Creative Writing Department of Seoul Arts University. He launched his literary career when two of his poems—"Good People" and "On That Day"—won the Annual Spring Literary Contest offered by the Hangook Ilbo in 1995.

Books of poetry:

> *You Are about to Go Somewhere*
> *Wind's Private Life*
> *Radiant*
> *Snowman Inn*
> *The Sea's Faring Well*
> *Parting Wants a Rendezvous with Me Today*

Selected books of prose:

> *Attraction*
> *Wind Blows; I Like You*
> *The One by My Side*
> *Oneself to Oneself*
> *And Then I Heard You Are Happy*

He has been recognized with the Prize for Contemporary Literature, the Discovery Literature Award, and the Park Jae Sam Literature Award. The literary coterie Poetry Power, of which he is a member, has been the hub of his poetic creativity.

About the Translator

Cho Young Shil holds a Master of English & English Literature from Chonnam University, Korea. A recipient of numerous grants for her English translation of modern Korean literature, she has translated and published nine contemporary Korean poetry books including *One Day, Then Another* by Kim Kwang-Kyu (White Pine Press, 2014), *Whisper of Splendor* by Chong Hyon-Jong (Homa & Sekey Books, 2018), *Forty Two Greens* by Chonggi Mah (Codhill Press, 2020), and *Bukchon* by Shin Dal Ja (Homa & Sekey Books, 2023).